Hope Is a Small Barn

Also By Gregory LeStage

Small Gods of Summer

Hope Is a Small Barn

Poems by

Gregory LeStage

Antrim House
Simsbury, Connecticut

Copyright © 2017 by Gregory LeStage

Except for short selections reprinted for purposes of
book review, all reproduction rights are reserved.
Requests for permission to replicate should
be addressed to the publisher.

Library of Congress Control Number: 2017938192

ISBN: 978-1-943826-29-2

First Edition, 2017

Printed & bound by Ingram, Inc.

Book design by Rennie McQuilkin

Front cover photograph by the author
Photograph on pp. iii and 1 by Sadie LeStage

Antrim House
860.217.0023
AntrimHouse@comcast.net
www.AntrimHouseBooks.com
21 Goodrich Road, Simsbury, CT 06070

to Chloë, Sadie, and Elsa,
who have grown up
knowing that words matter

Table of Contents

Words Matter / viii
Epigraph / x

I.

I Was So Ten / 4
Rescuing Mermaids / 7
Wave to Me / 9
Girl Playing Guitar / 10
Currency / 11
I Will Show You What Kestrels Do / 12
A Father Looks at 50 / 13
Frostfish Cove / 14
A Sky Spreads / 15
Ramshackle Paradise / 16
Benjamin B. Benjamin, Watchmaker / 17
Islands Passed / 19
Celebration / 20
To Keep Summer / 21
206 / 22

II.

The Magic Lantern / 28

III.

Milk Carton Kids / 40
Tracksides / 42
Some Thoughts for the Lord of a Once-Great House / 44
What Sanctuary / 45
No Child of His / 46
Oven-Haired / 47
Blood Betrayal / 48
Sinking with Stones / 49

Funeral Home / 53
Ashes-Talking / 54
Your Mother's Dress / 55
Turning the Ring / 56
Beacon / 58
At the Nursery / 59
Hope Is a Small Barn / 60
The Weather on Mother's Day / 61
Never Such Harmony / 62
Woodsmoke in Winter / 63

IV.

The Hunt / 66

About the Author / 74
About the Book / 75

WORDS MATTER

In the spring of 2009, a group of poets from Massachusetts gathered to identify and connect two persistent challenges, one affecting poetry and the other arts education. They shared proof that the community of poets across the state was fragmented, that poetry was distant from the lives of the public, that there was little access to accomplished poets, and that the art of poetry had retreated to the universities.

Of greatest concern was how poetry is being swept up in the reduction of arts education in schools. That concern deepened in 2010 when the Commonwealth cut fiction and poetry in schools by 60% and replaced them with Common Core's "informational texts." A 2016 editorial in *The Milford Daily News* entitled "Poetry Teaches More than Rhyme" examined how the removal of poetry from the curriculum would have a widespread negative effect on school children's literacy. Because of its relevance, this editorial went viral: it was re-printed and re-posted in many newspapers and sites across the state. This group of poets recognized that people of all ages and communities have little or no access to one of humankind's most ancient and essential art forms. However, they knew that the talent and energy necessary to address the situation were abundant. As a result, they created Mass Poetry to better the imaginative lives of our citizens, poets, students and teachers – and to contribute to arts education – by engaging people in the art of poetry. As of this writing, the organization engages approximately 300,000 people annually through its online presence and public programs.

I acknowledge any organization whose fundamental belief is that *Words Matter*. When combined into a poem, they can matter powerfully and beautifully. They move us to think, feel and act. To understand each other. At the present time in our country's history, I believe this matters more than ever before.

Gregory LeStage

If I'm somewhat academic (I'm more agricultural) and you are somewhat executive, so much the better: it is so we are saved from being literary and deployers of words derived from words.

Letter from Robert Frost to Wallace Stevens

Hope Is a Small Barn

I

I WAS SO TEN

I was so ten then –
bicycled, ram handle-barred, ten-speeded,
summering my way towards a not-far town.
My very setting out
startled all the world's spheres into motion,
so great was my journey.
I wheeled my hill-conquering route
under a twisting ribbon of starlings
blue angeling,
under seagulls bannering my name,
under wished-for weather
that mothered the salt pond and river.

Passing cars heroed
me with wide berth and handwaves, the roadside
bursting with bittersweet as I ivied
along and spooked egrets
ichabodding in eel grass. In earshot
were the hull-clapping bay,
the catboats mewling at moorings.
I rolled in the shower of my days, rays
or rain, coasted
into the general store for barrel-big
pickles and listening in
on the lilting lie traders just up

from the boatyard with
fresh tales of fish, fuel and wind. Only ice
cream parlored between me and the white church
federating whitely
at the crossroads, its headstones lichened and

lined up in parables,
the gauntlet of graves a pedal-
pumping shortcut past the oak, greatcoat gray,
lashed with lightning,
reeling on the heels of its roots from
the storm of my passings
to and through the siren street of girls

that had begun to
matter, biked on banana seats, pennants
of ponytails blowing straight out with speed,
halter-topped and flip-flopped
on porches and swings, legs dangling, hips on
easy swivels, all caught
in my weather eye now alert
for aunts in station wagons with cousins
in the wayback
tattling my doings on Main Street –
my doorway duckings sweet
with the penny cheap and forbidden.

I curled my copper
across the counter, bagged up the delights
– red hots, gumdrops, pop rocks – and took the road
at pace, trailing spindrift.
Dogged was I in the red hot noon.
Speed made my eyes turn crows
on fields into black flecks on green
and delivered me to trails steep, stumped and
canopied with
leaves, dappled down to the kettle pond,
where the trout-skin surface
sparkled and mottled me with wet light,

where the dark depths cooled
all ten of my growth rings. Then into the
warm wrinkled palm of the inlet cupping
the up-going tide, the
up-flying heron, or drawing the tide
and the heron's head down
into the vapors of dead low
seeping. Twilight drew the moth of me to
the ballpark, to
the picnicking crowd loud as lights, then
the race through the soldier's
cemetery, the Union undead

on my heels, their toy
tin replicas buried in my pocket,
the murmur and tang of moss at my back.
Downhill I javelined home
towards the gabled cottage beacon-bright,
past the reaching branches
of the spruce, beseeching and blue.
The moon, widow-walking the roof ridge, rose
in high relief
on my return. Spent I was as the
night air stung me, but my
body glowed mighty with my decade.

Now was time for the whip-poor-wills and owls,
whose tongues I spoke
from the ground nest of my bed and the pine
perch of my windowsill,
from where I oracled a boy's tomorrow.

RESCUING MERMAIDS

When an envy of mermaids
beached itself,
my daughters set about
rescuing them
from certain death
or something worse.
I suspect that they administered
a kind of serum
passed from hands to scales
in palmed cups of seawater.
No man can comprehend this,
of course.
Nor could I decode
what they spoke to the revived,
but figured it must have been
gentle dissuasion.
One by one, the flopping subsided
and they let themselves
be dragged seaward
by the hands,
their limp tails leaving trails
in the sand
and slicks of oil
flecked with glitter.
They sank at the surf line
with what must have been resignation.
I imagine that they recovered
under the breaking waves
and darted through kelp curtains

into the familiar.
Later, my girls reported
that they heard keening
while they were diving for shells.
They explained
that it was less a protest
than a peal of regret.

WAVE TO ME

From on top of the dune
I watched you do a wave dance
as if the teacher had said to the children
    Be the sea!
and released you to spin and twist
and make spray with your fingertips
running back and forth
    as naturally as possible
while I plotted our future.

GIRL PLAYING GUITAR

The
young
girl
sits
stick
straight
on a
chair,
a foil
to
her
guitar's
classic
shape.
The
curvaceous,
rosewood
Venus at leisure on the
lap of this lass needs the kind of
persuading that only a handmaiden
can provide, one who urges the body
to its side and begins the routine
cosseting with a gentle fret over
the neck. She soothes the strings
into a single note, stops to
tune when they complain. She
lays out matching chords, adorns them
with tremolos and triads. She pauses to fit a
capo necklace and is ready. Her green voice
begins to laurel and join her hollow goddess with
song. But she knows her station: she shyly lilts
slightly behind her lady, whose full-figured strums
divert attention from the girl's dropped tune, her
veering off to catch a stray note, to net a fluttering
lyric. Then she convinces her mistress to rest, and
this sudden acquiescence is the gift of *a cappella* as
the girl gives voice to the rising woman in her,
striving, soaring now, unaccompanied.

CURRENCY

Let's place our sand dollars
on the porch railing for a while
until the sun mints them in white.

Let's string them together
with fine, clear filament,
with fishing line,

so they will hang like coins caught
in the instant of dropping
from some high hand,

so they will imply
that we only spent them
on time.

I WILL SHOW YOU WHAT KESTRELS DO

Give me boyhood again,
and I will show you what kestrels do
in the tiffany of dusk,
on the concave of the wind,
holding the hover
over the meadow's lacework,
heir to what is about to happen,
everything finespun with intent,

and we will thread the lane
in short bursts of flight
to a house known to my compass,

and I will turn your ear towards
the distant ledge of the day,
where a red fox sends a yowl to itself
around the pine-rimmed bowl of the bay,

the answer that returns
no more or less changed
than what I have become to myself,
    woven, tapestried
then set aside,
until I admit
when it all comes back around
that I neither left nor arrived.

A FATHER LOOKS AT 50

to Chloë, Sadie and Elsa

Gather around and sing me your song of youth
so that I can tether my drifting truth
to the three-part harmony,
the honeyed braid of your voices.
You can neither see my entropy
nor helm my deep blue
   and its archipelago of cragged choices.

Strum in unison a single string
and send a sine wave to the ears of this king
when he needs to be drawn home
by music sweeter than the trill of the sirens
who entice him to roam
and look pastward in silence.

Lace the green reeds of your throats
into a wickerwork of notes –
today a pattern you begin to weave;
tomorrow a basket or a chair to hold me
when you must leave
and I am old and out to sea.

FROSTFISH COVE

Go down to Frostfish Cove
with all cares at your back
when the high tide
makes green scythe tips
of the marsh grass
and floats the tied dingy
for easy boarding.

Go down to Frostfish Cove
by the path through the woods
where bittersweet climbs
the scotch pine groves
in the briny breeze
and yellow jackets hive
in the leaf litter.

Go down to Frostfish Cove
across the field of timothy,
through the scribble of cabbage butterflies
and beneath the white oak
where the black dazzle
of assembling crows
gossips about your intent.

Go down to Frostfish Cove
from the ancient tract
where flint-cored farmers pushed
from the soil what the glacier left
then toiled seeds into rows
as the fishing ketches and tides
cycled at their backs.

A SKY SPREADS

Jamaica

A sky spreads its blue benediction
over hills that bow like nuns,
their black backs sweating blue vapors.

Bamboo spires in groves below the lolling buzzards
and above the coffee rose and shoeblack,
the yellow bellflower and sweet sap tree.

On the beach, the boatmen burn
whatever they find in fire kettles, pots and pits,
and think of the fish that may come,

while the roadside keepers of pocket-sized shops
await the Red Stripe delivery
and the breakdown of their jalopies.

In the clubs, the jobless drinkers clash and fight
over their shared plight,
harm-bringers afire with rum.

The ganja men sharpen and polish the blade,
meditating on revenge; they smoke to righteousness
then sleep, peaceful and crimeless.

We bud in the blue dusk, bloom when night teals,
then bleach in the cold moonlight
to start the morning white

in a place where
worry-hurry goes ta drown
an de sun hot like when fire ketch a town.

RAMSHACKLE PARADISE

for Elsa
Dunmore Town, Bahamas

The shingled shops and harbor huts ramshackle
and rim the sapphire sea, cahoot with the sun,
bargain with the breeze to stay standing, and cackle
with the beached boats that can't be bothered to float and run.

Stray cats dart from the road rooster's hackle
while the conch queen cleavers a choppy beat
and workmen spread the pink paint and spackle
on shanties of tin and pine where townsfolk meet
and pass in island ease through crooked doors
                            with neither latch nor shackle.

BENJAMIN B. BENJAMIN, WATCHMAKER

He is a maroon from St. Kitts making watches
in an expired town known for what its factories
spun into and out of gold, now reversed into flax.

Behind bowtie and three-piece suit, he lures you
into his shop with the flicker of his pearly minnow
mustache and a deft flash of his holstered handgun.

Held at punpoint, you are hostage to tall stories
told in a slanting lilt while the timepieces tick
like tiny bombs under glass and tock on the walls.

He sits watch and watches you watch the watches,
while he rhymes, waxes, pleads for his palm-rimmed island,
a colonizer in the dominion of talk.

He tools each beginning into a well-wrought wheel
and the pursuing paragraphs into pinions
that mesh to turn the mechanism of his craft.

I endure in a small manufacturing borough
with its white faces, gray snow, and muted mills
by daydreaming of my sun-soaked house,

my picture-perfect peninsula, and its vain, sugared past.
I lived on the east side wind that roughs up the sea
and pleats the coast, that seaward limit of the land.

I loved on the west side breeze that gently weaves
the harbor into smooth linen.
Always in the distance was Mount Misery

staring skyward with its dead-crater eye unblinking.
It is the Cyclops under whose blindness
I made solitary migrations through the elements.

My island brightly burnished me.
I'm a sand-and-salt-water-polished pirogue.
But I made my peregrination north,

and now I secrete over the grit inside my shell.
I am washed ashore, outcast,
but I'm in harmony with time and current.

Learn to long, to accept your marooned selves.
Lean in! Look at the movement!
More true than the tide!

ISLANDS PASSED

By now we have forgotten
what time of year
the star apples
come to juice,
the startling season
of the plum trees'
flowering and fruiting,
that month
when the ground doves
brown the fields
and the treacle
rises and reaches
in the sweet sap tree.
Our skin has no memory
of what moved across it
in buttery hushes,
of the light brown tattoo
we shared,
the warm sac of the sea.
There is no replaying
the guitar's *chikka*
in the offbeat,
the tethered goat's *maa*.
We cannot paint
the way the rain
rayed down in suddenness,
how the late sun
oranged the low clouds
in ribbons.
But someday we will map
the distant whoosh
of the surfaced porpoise
outside our night windows.

CELEBRATION

After I delivered your eulogy,
we adorned your vessel, set it ablaze,
then quaffed in a mead hall heavily
where I held court pridefully for the praise,
as you went to embers out of eyesight
and sank with a hiss – your final refrain,
one of us knowing I had done no more that night
than pluck and twist words in a daisy chain.

TO KEEP SUMMER

To keep summer from ending soon,
beg favors of the sun and moon.
Plead one to slow, one to sliver.
Bribe the sprites to hex the river
and fill it swollen as in June,
so the dusk will whirl without turning.

Grind a bushel of whelks to wampum.
Trade with natives for a precious sum,
for their elder's sway with the spirits
and the command of their secrets.
Chant and dance to their celestial drum,
so the sun will go without churning.

Invoke the sky to shower itself at night
with meteors that are instants in white.
Wear a necklace with an amber pendant
floating an ancient bee and resplendent
with its one kept moment of primal light,
so the dark will kindle without burning.

August yourself in that cool cornflower blue.
Spread your cobalt fingers in the drying dew
and lift them until they touch the height of noon.
Cut a handful quickly – press them very soon
in pages of a book you will return to.
So fades their color, so goes the yearning.

206

to Julia

What I can guarantee
is that when all of me that is soft
has fallen away in peels,
shingled off in flakes,
and shrunk into curls of gristle
on their way to oblivion,
a hard substance
in a precise number will remain
as my final will and testament.

Disarticulate me
into 206 parts
so that I can say what I mean,
become what I meant.
Scatter my bones
in bars and basements,
ball fields and bilges
where they will absorb the damp
of the spilled drinks, the bluegrass and clay,
the pooled seawater
and ignite the spontaneous rearrangement
of their crystalline matrix.
Let the collagen speak for me
in its fibrous tongue and calcium alphabet,
its protein rune.

Blazon the oceanfront
with my 52 foot bones and their 66 joints

– just below the high tide line
where they once anchored me.
The gulls will make meals of the marrow,
the hermit crabs homes
of the hollowed knuckles.
An epoch's worth of currents
will polish a few of them in the gyre
and gift one or two
to an eventual beachcomber.
They will speak again
from some sea-facing porch,
hanging from a driftwood mobile
and jangling with bells of shells
and found fossils.

Inlay a femur in the paved bitumen
cul-de-sac of my boyhood.
Leave a basketball, chalk, and transistor radio
beneath the sagging backboard and rusting hoop,
but not too close to the ruins
of dinnertime.

Hide my elbow bones
in the arid book stacks on the highest floor
of the library near that dim-lit desk
where they served
their head-propping purpose.

Inside the cab of my ancient Chevy pickup,
where everything was slower
and smelled of what you now know
was a sweet, musty never,

clack and slap my two rib bones together
or tap them on the metal dash
to the beat of the songs that play
between the local ads
and the over-telling of time
on the AM radio.
Leave them in the glove compartment
next to the ivory dice.

Place three tiny ossicles
in three silver lockets for my girls
to wear around their necks
as reminders that I listened.
In the bedrock of these ear bones
is the veined ore
of what they said to me
now deposited into lodes
not eroded by the waters
of what I said to them
over all those years.

Set your expectations
of what will happen
to the bones you bury in soil
where the acid is high,
like where bullying or betrayal happened.
Their undoing will be faster.
No fading whimper of decomposition,
but a collapsing surrender of my stones
in slow motion miniature.

Although I cannot guide you to the base
of the right hill to place my skull
because I could not choose between
my Jerusalems,
never staked out
a Golgotha in any outskirts,
you must not leave it nowhere.
That is, in the end,
if you confess to yourself
that I was a stranger,
then do not deposit me
in the treasury between your temples.
Just buy a potter's field and
bury it there.
But, if I was known and knowable,
then sink my skull in a peat bog
for discovery in some millennium
when scientists will extract
precisely what it thought and felt.

II

THE MAGIC LANTERN

I love my life's dark hours
In which my senses quicken and grow deep,
While, as from faint incense of faded flowers
Or letters old, I magically steep
Myself in days gone by: again I give
Myself unto the past: again I live.

– Rilke

i.

Even at rest in your favorite chair
after an affirming day plying your trade,
you were in throes of the Doppler Effect:
your experience of the sound
of what was always coming at you
was much higher, sharper and louder
than that same sound as it moved away from you.
This was an ordeal you endured in private.
You lived as a hurtling ellipsis,
a forward-falling spiral,
but knew that you weren't built for speed,
the speed of all things now,
or for a life pushpinned with depots,
never destinations.
At what point did you pull the brake handle,
grind to a halt and reverse the journey
to recover yourself?

ii.

Maybe you embarked from a vision of yourself in bed
drifting backward through the gauze of near-sleep

as the headlights from the road arrowed
across your wall and struck
your great-grandfather's stereopticon
– the magic lantern –
and set off a projection of images,
scatterlings begging for a place in the narrative
from the verges of a half-lit path:
the bristle-chinned babysitter
in her house dress and wingtips;
some spinster's melancholy breath
curdling in a heatwave;
the agony lit by the downy hair
lying down then standing up
on the mother's face
over and over in some autumn zephyr;
the flung chum of the pet rabbit
strewn across the lawn, and the culprit hound
with his winsome lips and pitiful eyes;
the mercy-killed cat and euthanized uncle.

iii.

Did you thresh a merciful boyhood
from the recollection of that one day
when you were enraptured
by an exquisite luna moth marooned in the sunlight
and scrawling its plot lines
above an arrangement of lilies,
a fevered *pas de deux* in greens and whites,
and then despondent at nightfall
when witnessing at the window as it repeatedly
rushed the pyre of the porch light
like some demented new widow?

Or did the fixedness of your rearward gaze
winnow husks of certainty from grains of doubt
about who you really were that day?
After all, you were aroused
by the frozen flutter of its wings
and the stilled feathers of its antennae
when it later hovered in ethanol sacrifice,
exquisitely pinned to a cork bed
in a glass-covered box.
Those moments are projected back to you
in a triptych of passion, ravage and qualm –
three panels that hang uncurated in your past.
Your search opens and closes them on their hinges.

iv.

Perhaps what wrecked you
was the hall light's sudden betrayal
of the pistoning buttocks in the bedroom
that set off those too-early stirrings in the loins,
the kind that cast you headlong and insensate
down blind alleys and dry culverts
where there was nothing for you,
not even questions.

And what about the fact
that no one in your house
would call death by its name?
It shapeshifted into idioms
that lodged in your ear
and lozenged into words you couldn't spit out.
Most nights, the Brothers Grimm
benignly dropped crumbs of allegories

under your blanket.
With your contraband flashlight,
you trailed them across the pages
but always fell asleep benighted.

You only saw an actor in cameo
when you peered through the aperture
of your grandfather's missing eye
or at the tight, white bayonet scar on his temple,
at his paintings of the field
where he should have bled out and burned up
among the matchheads of poppies,
at the grim poetry he recited
from the slim volume of his remembrance.
Soon it was your turn to put on a uniform
and stand alone and exposed
in a field blazing with dandelions.
On your back was stitched a number,
on the front the name of the local funeral home,
the sponsor of your Little League team.
While you saw limited action
in your right field outpost,
you felt the honor that came with a uniform
for which thousands had to die
so that you could wear those polyester pinstripes,
that adjustable cap.
Such dawnings about death
became precarious and then sudden,
like very nearly falling backward in a tipped chair.

All the while, there was no intuition
about the nautilus that sea-whispered
from your red bookshelf.
Although you wore its surface smooth over the years

studying the pearly septa of its chambered shell,
the depression of its whorl sections,
the sinuousness of its sutures,
although you wondered about its tubular siphuncle
being long gone from its halls,
you were dumb to the golden secret of its spiral.
But the magic lantern tells no story:
its two lenses merely display pictures
in two dimensions,
one dissolving while the next is forming.
This is before your mind invented moving pictures.

v.

The coming of age was the splicing
of awareness and structure into a reel
that you wound forward in plot lines.
You even found a logic in the twists and reversals.
Later, you were able to narrate
the salad days of your documentary
and the sequence of your middle age
over cocktails or dinner
without referring to the script.
But when everyone else went to bed
you took out the double ledger
and tried to account for what had fluttered
to the cutting room floor
so that you could story yourself to yourself.
You made no further entries.

vi.

And then an epiphany:
rhapsody struck when you learned
that the nautilus' spiral whirls
away from its center point
by the exact same factor
for every quarter turn it takes.
That this pristine *phi*
is the common geometry of life itself.
When you cracked the cipher, you instantly felt
its handiwork in the architecture of your bones.
There was bliss when you took a compass and straightedge
to the sunflower's seed pattern
and a telescope to the galaxy and confirmed it:
all structures, forms and proportions
cosmic or individual, organic or inorganic,
acoustic or optical, have the same blueprint.
But the feeling was fleeting.
Your final concession – that this golden ratio
would never reveal its arithmetic –
was a knifing in broad daylight:
those god damned decimals arched into infinity
without ever repeating themselves.
Accepting the endlessness of your search
was the twisting of the knife.

vii.

The taking of your marital vows
was the dropping of an anchor.
Later, their retaking a mooring
with a chain linked by two hands holding,

and holding fast your bed
when it rocked, settled, floated.
Children brought you up,
family cropped up,
friends shored you up.
The birth of your first grandchild
was a moon tide that raised you up,
left salt on your palms from weeping
that you later tasted and savored.
These people lived lightly on your land,
slowly consecrating it with their abiding presence –
walking on it, rutting shortcuts through the woods,
sweeping clouds from the skies with kites,
keeping the fields clear, leaving some space wild.
They burned, planted, watered, mowed.
They lay in the grass alone and together,
faces up and faces down.
They opened their veins to your ground.
You were joined.

viii.

But Pygmalion still hectored you in quiet moments,
usually just before dawn
or on long, caffeinated drives in the non-hours.
You knew his tale –
that he avoided the village women
by sculpting Aphrodite over and over
in small clay figurines, buying time by
seeking the perfect pose.
Falling in love with the finished statue

saved him from female flesh and bond.
When he finally goaded you
to caress the S-curves
of the Medici Venus' half-clad torso,
what did you read on the stone of her skin?
Did you pity her partial state – and yours?
You kept her bakelite statuette hanging
from your rearview mirror as a swinging reminder.
You haunted newsstands
for their top-shelf offerings
and rifled through your yearbooks
to find the faces of the one-night stands.

ix.

At some point, you realized
that there would be no payoff
for all those nightfalls spent
embalming your deceased hours
with pine pitch, myrrh and the resin of recall.
They all just dried into distilled essences of old proteins,
strips of keepsake jerky in your pocket.
Eventually, you were able to accept
that you were not recapturing lost time
but only writing a history
of the way you always felt about lost time.
You even admitted shooting your various periods
in different aspect ratios
only in order to evoke earlier phases
of your own storytelling.
It was all just metonymy.

x.

When you sensed that it could be a state of being
in which you were suspended,
serous fluid in an amnion,
your journey angled toward its purpose.
You then divined that it is a place,
perhaps a splendid hotel
like one of those you frequented in Provence
in the halcyon days.
Everything there is composed but animate,
even the air with its lavender hint.
The flowers at reception are always fresh.
Sun rays flute into the clear-watered vases
and disperse themselves in a spectrum
that papers the walls.
The décor tailors itself to the light –
accents with shadows –
and the setting is your state of mind.
Guests are hosts; hosts are guests.
Everyone is related by blood or something thicker.
The space is designed to incite love or its repair.
Intimacy concertinas in the arbor and by the pool.
All your needs are met before you know you have them.
You, too, are a meeter of needs.
Your presence completes the tableau.
Sadness is there, too, cooing from a cage
in the lobby near all those vases
and pecking at millets of solace.
And death, a permanent visitor with a routine,
walks the halls because you did not turn it away,
because you accepted it,
indeed, because you invited it into an accord.
In return, it frees you to be

intensely present on the veranda
where you can see beyond the view,
where you can hear the cogs of the bougainvillea
cycling starch and water in its leaves
and mixing its magenta.
Death's kinship emboldens you
to inhabit time
with supreme presence,
soaring awareness,
effortless openness to beauty and cruelty,
secret grace and towering stupidity,
ham-fisted faith and unwelcome truth,
blatant decay and cell-level uncertainty;
to understand that each instant
contains all those that preceded it
and the atoms of those to come,
an expanding universe of moments;
that what lasts and links
are the leavings of love
you got and gave, give and get –
a bodiless embrace, not a clutch or cling,
imageless and without sequence;
that things fall together,
free of story.

III

MILK CARTON KIDS

We were all milk carton kids back then.
In some state of being snatched.
Before, during, after.

We went missing
from perfect hometowns,
the kind rimmed with farms,
and town greens with cannons,
and Friday night football,
and earnest PTAs
with vigilance on the agenda.

We went missing
at kitchen tables
sitting squarely
in front of our parents,

who were long oblivious to the signs,
like the silence,
the one-word answers,
the sketchy friends,
the hair-trigger pout,

who could report
with earnest precision
our height, weight,
eye and hair color,
dates of birth,
but were never quite sure
about our dates
of disappearance.

We came back many years later
as parents,
the porous surface of our memories
wiped clean by the methylate
of siring and birthing,
having forgotten
that the missing were mostly there,
the present seldom seen,
that you can't look for what you don't miss,
that we once would rather have been
shattered than hollow,
broken than empty.
That nothing we know matters more
than what never happened.

Now we see
the gable-topped cartons as miniatures
of the houses we vanished from,
our faces staring out of the paperboard window,
Have you seen me?
stamped in flexo-graphic print on the paperboard sill.

TRACKSIDES

When there was no more poetry
in the rail yards and sidings
where
rolling stock rolls
and freight freights,
nor in the spaces between
the stations, junctions and switching yards
beyond the view or care
of the yardmasters and switchmen,
the car knockers and wheel tappers,
where tampers and ghosts of gandy dancers
perform for the hobos and move on,

we turned to the terrain
that deadens along the way
from the fence to the ditch,
the ditch to the batter slope
and slides into a nameless margin
between all that and the rails,
where the spilled and dumped
atomize in the train's frozen wake,
where the tract's rough upper lip
puckers against the ass ends
of homes squatting in hollows
in hard luck abutment,
where the land lies stripped and prone
to the acned backs
of warehouses lined up
to be passed by at speed,
written off by graffiti,

that writ of the defunct,
that coroner's signature in bright colors,

and followed it far out
into wide-open country
where it just runs on
in negative space,
a dumb accomplice to the track's
sermon on vastness.

Along the way,
we used whatever words we wanted
to name or describe it
so long as they conjured
the act just before stillness,
then the stillness.

When we came upon
an untracked locomotive
in a shaded spur,
parted out,
tilting and dismantling
under the torch of time,
the muscled torque of gravity,
we discovered the aftermath
of still,
and a new word-stock
spilled out before us.

SOME THOUGHTS FOR THE LORD
OF A ONCE-GREAT HOUSE

Minster Lovell, c. 1430, Oxfordshire, England

My daughters play at damsels and maidens
in the rough ruins of your ancient hall.
I ponder how such a great height descends;
they climb the crags and dance a phantom ball.

Demesne, villein, lush fields, and some king's grace
fused to form and brace your limestone backbone.
Children decorated the chambered space,
but the seeds of collapse you must have sown.

Suspecting your vice cankered the mortar,
I reject any forfeit, fire or scourge
that could have left you no choice, no quarter –
then, in the light, catch myself on the verge.

Who's not but one misfortune from the end,
from dooming what matters to roam the rubble and pretend?

WHAT SANCTUARY

And what sanctuary those places
where saints-in-wanting cruise
in quadrangles of contained dark and light,
in cloisters where black gives way to white
when the sun during visitation
looks into the arches then turns away
and gives back the shadows
and what happens in them,
in pulpits under glass stained bright
and opaque with the oily soot
of preaching,
in vestries blackened
by the twisting of sins into secrets
and where secrets are guttering candles
throwing shapes on the vestments,
visions flickering and false?

NO CHILD OF HIS

He once wished for a child with raven hair,
almond-curved eyes and a deep onyx stare,
an open, earth-and-olive-tinted face
alight with the sun of some other place.

OVEN-HAIRED

Oven-haired and linoleum-lipped
she knifes down the interstate,
her face a stolen car,
the wisp of her mutterings
the wind of wasp wings,
the phantom limb
throbbing in her trunk,
her tongue the needle
sewing the severed sinew
of conversation that had held
the bones of them together.

BLOOD BETRAYAL

*Mama don't understand it,
she wants to know where I've been.
I'd have to be some kind of natural born fool
to want to pass that way again.*

– James Taylor

What she wouldn't give for a long, dirt road,
some broken-in boots and a cool, dry breeze
to take her away from what you have sowed.

She should have slipped out after you harrowed
peace with treason and put her on her knees.
What wouldn't she give for a long, dirt road?

She should have seen sooner what you furrowed.
There need be but one more dark act she sees
to take her away from what you have sowed.

The way would be downhill; she'd have no load,
would ramble beyond earshot of your pleas.
She wouldn't give *what* for a long, dirt road?

You would scan the horizon while she crowed
Abandon and sang herself new stories
to take her away from what you have sowed.

Her inkling of black shoots grasping, of rows hoed
with ire in her absence finally foresees
what she would give for a long, dirt road
to take her away from what you have sowed.

SINKING WITH STONES

Roberta F. Foote (1939-2015)

i.

DIVING FOR PEARLS

This is the line that turns her tumor stone
into a hewn granite weight in her grip,
and her into a sleek pearl diver
descending expertly
into any shallow shoal or
soft opal sea of her liking.

She chooses
some far-flung Pacific peninsula
where the Japanese *Ama* prosper,
the sea women,
rulers of the thick forests
of arame seaweed,
hunters of abalone,
those soft-meated,
closed keepers of candescence.

She can dive on her own,
motionless and vertical,
but cannot rise alone.
Every pearler needs her puller,
every puller a purpose.
This is the line that turns her catheter
into a hempen cord.
Around her waist

and secured to the skiff's gunwale,
a lifeline held by the sure hand
that she once held in her own,
that used to grasp her apron string,
that now wears a ring
and holds small hands of its own,
a hand that is her reason
to keep her one lungful,
to release her stone,
to tug on the cord,
to seize and rise,
to trust the lift
that is the filial law of duty,
that the devoted hands in the boat
will help her ascend
from every descent.

This is the line between
the brine and the air and the light,
the one that must break
so that she can surface,
softly exhale her sea whistle,
present her string bag brimming
with chances of answers,
tilt her head sunward
with wisdom about where to return
over and over,
for however long
her forever lasts.

ii.

A THEORY OF DISPLACEMENT

When the tumor stone
made her heavier
than the warm liquid existence
that had floated her since birth,
she sank
displacing all of it on the way down.

The fluid mechanics of her descent
were set in motion
whirling and spinning those who loved her
into vortices of lament,
into worrying maelstroms
set off by the sinking object of herself
and pushing them into empty places,
rooms with shades drawn,
dawn docksides, open fields.

Scans and dyes revealed only a mass
of facts, not equations or quotients of weights.
No newtons or multipliers,
no scale to measure what was displaced.
Nothing divisible by anything.
Even her intimates,
who swore they knew her utterly,
could not deduce her volume.

Until she came to rest at the bottom,
we refused to accept
that there was no upward buoyant force,

no upthrust of oncology
equal to her density,
to her stone
now multiplied into strewn stones,
into masses of axioms,
into a theorem proven, fixed, still.

And then the truth-tide of morphine.
It flooded her veins,
coursed through her conscience
and flushed the secrets
out of her mouth.
Tongue freed
she mind-gushed,
truth-sluiced,
jettisoned false ballast,
made flotsam of the classified,
jetsam of the confidential,
and her mass became less
than what she had displaced.

Up she rose lighter,
enlightened and enlightening,
ascending into amnesty,
going to gossamer through others' grace,
others' compassion quickening her conversion to carbon,
suspending the physical law of buoyancy
to break the surface as vapor
and release us
from our unquiet qualm,
from our bobbing and treading.

FUNERAL HOME

"It is our experience that the most devoted families select the Director's Cremation Package."

Removal from the place of parting
Medical examiner and associated fees
Cremation casket of finished birch
All paperwork in certified copies
Your choice of church
Solid marble urn or chest
Hearse to the crematory
Printed materials for each guest
Limousine to and from the cemetery
Music before and after service is concluded
Acknowledgement cards as traditional
Government permit filing included
Newspaper charges additional
Staff at the door to assist the departing

ASHES-TALKING

for Julia

The moment before the phone rang
and knelled the news of your orphaning,
you felt your double helix shift and pang,
as if someone shook your ladder from the bottom,
as if, in the tunnels beneath your heart,
the spirits pealed the bells of your atoms
to tell you it was their time to depart.

When the his-and-hers ashes arrived in tupperware
on our doorstep in a box with the mail,
you placed the two containers in the willow ware
tureen your mother filled with consommé at Christmas.
You enshrined it in our kitchen,
a ceramic sarcophagus
at rest on a black marble slab above the trash bin.

That room now doubles as a tomb
you grace with classical gifts for the dead:
milk, honey, wine, flowers potted and in bloom.
They are luminous among the groceries.
You interrogate the ashes about their dark deeds,
regale them with daily joys, confide gentle mercies,
while flipping through your catalogs of clothes and unmet needs.

You do not know that ashes-talking in a catacomb
is a rite as old as foreign wars, burned bodies
and the blood bond that brings them home
in urns and pots, jars and coffers.
You are running your words through their dust like fingers
seeking something solid, sifting for answers,
or just for grains of an essence that still lingers.

YOUR MOTHER'S DRESS

She's wearing it in the color photograph,
mid-stride across the courtyard
of a philanthropist's chateau
or some ambassador's terrace.

The hemline is the era's,
the neckline of her own design.
Her calf, raised and taut,
positions the kitten heel

to strike the cobblestone chord perfectly.
The horizon line, epic in the background,
serves her purpose.
She appears so comfortable in it,

so charmed and charming.
The light and the lens conspire
to match it to her eyes just then,
which is certainly why she bought it –

for that event,
so that grace and gravitas
would promenade on the pinhead
of that snapped second,

of the aperture that limits the quantity of light
on who she is,
now a revealed shard of her civility,
of her self.

Today, it slouches
on a hanger in your closet,
except when you open all the windows
to make it move in the breeze.

TURNING THE RING

I was struck by your attentiveness
when I was talking to you the other night,
by the new language your body was speaking,
by the way your chin didn't tilt away,
the newly-stilled eyebrow, held gaze,
that question or two.
I noted that an open, upward-facing palm
had replaced the fist in your pocket.

During your time away, you changed yourself
to suit all those requests
we had prepared but never voiced,
that you were now clairvoyant to.

You sat on the edge of my bed
and meditatively turned
the ring on my finger as I slept.
The nurse had eased it off yours with vaseline,
placed it in an empty pill bottle,
and presented it to me for wearing.
A hushed and sterile ceremony.
A new prescription.

I had long watched you turn
steering wheels and helms,
spigots, thermostats and clock keys,
tides of talk, tables of doubt.

But this was a different turning,
counter-clockwise and rueful,
then clockwise and resigned.

I didn't get the feeling you were trying
to twist it off, to reclaim it.
Perhaps you had discovered
that gold lacked value
where you were.

BEACON

When the holidays became inevitable,
a friend took an off-ramp from his trip
between prodigy and prodigal
to visit his father in his hometown.

He recalls that snowflakes were flipping
in the dark like lit-up playing cards
when he returned to an even darker house
after a night out with his old crowd.

Listing and groping in the front hall,
he took a bearing from a tiny beacon
at the end of the unlit passage,
in the den.

An orange ember hovered,
then described a slow, perfect arc
from low to high
and stopped to illuminate
a downturned face and two waiting lips.

AT THE NURSERY

When we visit the nursery
I am drawn to the conifers,
dwarfed and shaped,
always green,
then to the cineraria and other
silvering plants
that last the winter,
until you show me
the colored forms
that look like a child's idea
of how a flower should look
in its brief, bright moment.

HOPE IS A SMALL BARN

Triolet

Hope is a small barn I have raised,
the roof half open to the sky.
The rain poured in; in the sun blazed.
Hope is a small barn I have raised,
with a chance to stand or be razed.
Where you stand it's wet or warm. My
hope is a small barn. I have raised
the roof half open to the sky.

THE WEATHER ON MOTHER'S DAY

The weather does not matter now.
It is not the day to pull the plow.
You will rise for a day of rest
and arc and set in the west
watching what your rain
did for your seed, your wind to your vane;
knowing that your snow was a throw,
a blanket that you thawed when it was time to grow
under your shine and blaze;
surveying what you raised,
what you made green and bright,
what today turns toward your light.

NEVER SUCH HARMONY

Never such harmony at home
as when our place and our people
join at the violet hour
and make and break bread
beneath a sheltering sky
under a star-strung strand of tiny lights
when each savory word
gets its just desserts in sweet reply,
while the glasses chime the time
and laughter is the subject and the object,
where conversation warms
the irises of eyes
until they bloom, internally lit,
then bouquet into affection
when they lean towards the candlelight.

After the moon and the jazz,
the carillon of peepers in the pond,
and the rosining of crickets' bows
have wheeled us onward,
after the fireflies have flicked
their lighters in the crowd,
and the June bugs have clung
to the screen doors
for their last swig of lampshine,
we find ourselves
in the awaited province of the night
to which we have traveled
so that honesty,
that nocturnal thing,
will come to eat from our hands.

WOODSMOKE IN WINTER

A scent of woodsmoke in winter
is an anamnesis on the wind
stirring someone older than ancient,
someone we all once were,
some child or safe self long gone.

An ash in the air,
a loose leaf of cinder,
a kiting hint of a place
from which to leave and return
assured of a rock or a stool or a chair

where we can linger and hear
the timber's last exhale
and warm ourselves in its offering,
its final release of stored light.

IV

THE HUNT

By the time I joined the hunt, it was ancient
and eternalized by millennia of spoor:
footprints, nests of boughs, possible scat.

No hunter was handpicked, no tracker dragooned:
we were self-draftees, some of us goateed
with satchels full of high school sleights,
notepads with pencilled grudges,
with inventions for seeing around corners,
with fathers in tow and long dead.

Some were stooped and stubborn from years
of studying manuals and barely losing arguments.
All of us trammeled but undamned,
let fly to chase and reify
by a triggered chromosome and notions of lack.

We moved together less like starlings
and more like a loose affiliation of kin
necklaced with binoculars and cameras,
strapped with crossbows and carbines.

Down the ages, our forefathers had vouchsafed
scratchings on parchment and sketches on vellum.
They had scrawled lists on index cards,
left them for us in safety deposit boxes,
crannied them in walls of hideouts and humidors.
What they traced gave contour to our prey,
but without color or punctuation
were just smudged guesswork,
flackspeak boast-filtered through bourbon.

We rambled down the meltwater braids
of the outwash plains
and swifted the wide-ridged moraines.
We prowled the glacial till,
the kettled and knolled countryside
poking sticks into holes
and volleying our voices into caves
because, sometimes, the beast was almost there.

I might have been the fleetest among us,
the best suited to snow and sand,
my arches still holding up.
I had the practiced squint of the plainsman,
the guile of the obsidian trader,
and a knack for playing the carom.
But my hesitant hands were those of a failed surgeon,
were hidden in deerskin gloves, in a diversion of fists.
Still, I knew where to get whale oil,
how to attach a lyric to a song and staunch tears,
to fletch a memory and sharpen its point.
And I burned optimism in a lantern,
which served us well during eclipses of hope
and when moons quandaried us in yellow.

We tended to skirt fens and bogs,
were drawn to evergreen copses on hillocks
where the high cover cloaked our surveillance.
The soft soil of the forest floor,
with its mosses, liverwort and lichen,
bedded us on our backs in an effervescence of balsam.
It sapped from us light talk of dark matter
under the patter of dropping cones.
Our words rose through the houses of the evergreens
and into the rafters and lofts of their branches.

They sparrowed themselves in the eaves of the canopy,
a safe distance from our understory,
from our years spent on dark talk of light matters,
when the hunt was still hearsay.

A high hill sunrise once blossomed a view of a town
where one of us had an aunt who let us bivouac
on the rim of her paddock
so that we could smell its morning breath
in the mist and make plans.
We paid her restitution by listening
to her hunt-widow's story of silence
as the colorless, odorless gas seeping
through the crumbling foundation
of her home life,
as the taste of old pennies in her mouth,
the lead in her waters.

Mostly, though, the women looked at us
with the kind of pity reserved
for the tamed and the bilked,
though their magazines explained everything.

The young shared spyglasses with the old
and watched us with want
as we flooded the meadows
with the menace of our intent.

We would turn to pillaging middens
when starved for the leftovers of kitchen life.
Candle ends that once fluttered light so fond
and rinds that once cased the mists of citrus
– when talk and taste were close–
became charms pocketed for fondling.

One time, children's voices feathered over us
in a flight of pheasants beaten from the low scrub;
their wings spun coils of memory behind them
and brushed our faces with intimacy.
Now, as then, we cried their cries
and accepted they were grown and gone.

We avoided sports grounds
after one of us once broke down and raved at the gate
about a missed hurdle or a dropped pass
that ruined everything for him, even his marriage.
When the constable came to investigate,
we hunkered in the gloaming,
disgraced like dimed-out vandals,
and agonized again when the creature
slipped a sneer into the birdsong just for us.

Sometimes we aced like falcons
over bog holes and fell fields,
took chattermarks by leaps and
cleared cinder cones by bounds.
At our best, we laced our way
through jackstraw timber
in a miasma of determination
thrumming with happenstance.
Too often, though, we only found
where a body had just been
in a corner of some wild moorland.
Nothing was ever there,
only steam wisping in a tease above the grass
flattened, cupped, still warm.

At one such point,
my spirit stilled then distilled into dispirit;

I couldn't take it anymore and peeled away from the pack,
taking stock and withdrawing across a floodplain
wreathed with loop after loop of wandering channels
that doubled back on themselves
and babbled *no, no, no* to forders and followers.
The men squatted in a tumbled column and watched me go
with the prescience of fortune cookie writers,
wordlessly warning that loneliness kills.
I slid into a gully, slept in a frost hollow,
and plotted my route to the sea,
where I knew it would be.

*

In and out of seasons, I walked deer paths
and palimpsests of trade routes,
dirt tracks and sheep trails.
Sabbath bells within earshot
and monasteries in silhouette
were the closest I came to desertion.

I fed crusts to curs and flipped coins to buskers,
expected postcards in return
for those I hadn't written
from villages I hadn't visited.

I had to hum past the almshouses
to block out the sound of ladles on aluminum,
to deny that I belonged there
among the fallen and flaccid, the toupeed and tongue-tied.

I began to work the wharves
because I sensed that it would seek cover
near men on the edge,

that it could turn to mimicry
and match itself to the backdrop
of cranes and cargo, bravado and bluster.

I looked for scratch marks on pilings and piers,
while the hunching net-menders looked the other way.
I could neither pick the locks of the stevedores' jaws,
nor cotton to the longshoremen's booze-baited tales
of wraiths who put them in thrall to daily drownings
and of the sway of that gypsy, time,
who promised this, but delivered that.

I had lost the scent,
fallen short of the outer edge.

*

A day or so east of the outermost
a shoreline unfurled before me in a flecked fabric
the color of skin and bone.

I dug into a dune,
made myself blind to all things and waited
as the dusk miracled around me in umber,
and the beachgrass held me
in its web of creeping underground stems,
its promise to thrive under shifting conditions.

With the crossing over to instinct came soft singing,
then the lyring of my voice to whatever felt like notes,
and the cosseting of an ache born of solitude.

I began to make my peace with all
that I could never understand

by reckoning through the archive of the inexplicable –
why the drowning surrender bittersweetly,
why the god-mixed alchemy of the placenta
smells like earth and salt,
why man loves pity more than love –
when something startled the sandpipers,
sent them up in a firework of darting and twisting.
They flashed their white underwings
in the sinking sun and in precise unison,
mirrors glinting me a Morse code message of presence.

I rose above the blind and saw the thing there,
ankle-deep in a tidal pool,
billowing and bending,
arching and straightening its back
with an affect of distance and blur:
near then far, far then near
like a dream flickering out
in the trickling douse of a morning.

It stood proof-angled between me and the sunset.
I loaded with compassion,
took aim with a resolve that felt like deliverance and,
when it turned to go in stride or slither,
shot it
on film.

*

The burden of proof was on me.
Self-appointed experts pored
over the technical characteristics of the footage,
the filming speed, the morphology of the creature.
They made detailed analyses of its biomechanics

and cited its ponderous momentum,
the sagging of what might have been a knee
as weight came onto it.

They annotated its confident, unwavering exit –
deeming it neatly expressive but open-ended,
ultimately inconclusive, like faith.
And it was the faith claims
that flamed the hoax-shamers.
Schoolchildren only saw the low-water whirlpool
left by the hasty twist of a foot or hoof
and the brute shadow on the ripples,
which clergymen divined as my own.

A letter from a man,
who conscientiously objected to the hunt,
shared evidence of vestigial wings
and proposed a devolved archangel.

My wife saw nothing whatsoever.

Gregory LeStage lives in Jamaica Plain, Massachusetts with his wife of twenty-five years and three daughters. He is a former academic who left university life long ago for the challenges of the business world and is currently a senior executive at a large global management consulting firm. His passions include an old farmhouse on Cape Cod, his workshop and tools, and antique vehicles. He earned his PhD and Master's from Oxford University and his BA from Trinity College in Hartford, CT. His poems have appeared in a number of publications; and his articles, interviews and reviews have been published by *Poetry Review, the Times Literary Supplement, Times Higher Education Supplement, New Writing, Notes & Queries,* and *Oxford Today*. His first poetry collection, *Small Gods of Summer*, was published by Antrim House in 2013 and was a finalist for the Eric Hoffer Prize.

This book is set in Garamond Premier Pro, which had its genesis in 1988 when type-designer Robert Slimbach visited the Plantin-Moretus Museum in Antwerp, Belgium, to study its collection of Claude Garamond's metal punches and typefaces. During the mid-fifteen hundreds, Garamond—a Parisian punch-cutter—produced a refined array of book types that combined an unprecedented degree of balance and elegance, for centuries standing as the pinnacle of beauty and practicality in type-founding. Slimbach has created an entirely new interpretation based on Garamond's designs and on compatible italics cut by Robert Granjon, Garamond's contemporary.

To order additional copies of this book
or other Antrim House titles, contact the publisher at

Antrim House
21 Goodrich Rd., Simsbury, CT 06070
860.217.0023, AntrimHouse@comcast.net
or the house website (www.AntrimHouseBooks.com).

•

On the house website
in addition to information on books
you will find sample poems, upcoming events,
and a "seminar room" featuring supplemental biography,
notes, images, poems, reviews, and
writing suggestions.